FROM THE DESKTOP OF JEFFREY SIMMONS

A vacation in Paris inspired Miroslav Sasek to create childrens travel guides to the big cities of the world. He brought me *This is Paris* in 1958 when I was publishing in London, and we soon followed up with *This is London*. Both books were enormously successful, and his simple vision grew to include more than a dozen books. Their amusing verse, coupled with bright and charming illustrations, made for a series unlike any other, and garnered Sasek (as we always called him) the international and popular acclaim he deserved.

I was thrilled to learn that *This is Washington, D.C.* will once again find its rightful place on bookshelves. Sasek is no longer with us (and I have lost all contact with his family), but I am sure he would be delighted to know that a whole new generation of wide-eyed readers is being introduced to his whimsical, imaginative, and enchanting world.

YOUR NAME HERE

THIS IS
WASHINGTON, D.C.

UNIVERSE

M. Sasek

This is
Washington, D.C.

Published by arrangement with Simon & Schuster Books for Young Readers,
Simon & Schuster Children's Publishing Division

This edition first published in the United States of America in 2011
by Universe Publishing,
A Division of Rizzoli International Publications, Inc.
300 Park Avenue South
New York, NY 10010
www.rizzoliusa.com

Text and pictures copyright © Miroslav Sasek, 1969
Illustrations on pages 60-63 by Jessie Hartland

*See updated Washington, D.C. facts at the end of the book

2011 2012 2013 2014 / 10 9 8 7 6 5 4 3 2 1

Printed in China

ISBN-13: 978-0-7893-2232-6

Library of Congress Catalog Control Number: 2010939760

Cover design: Sara E. Stemen

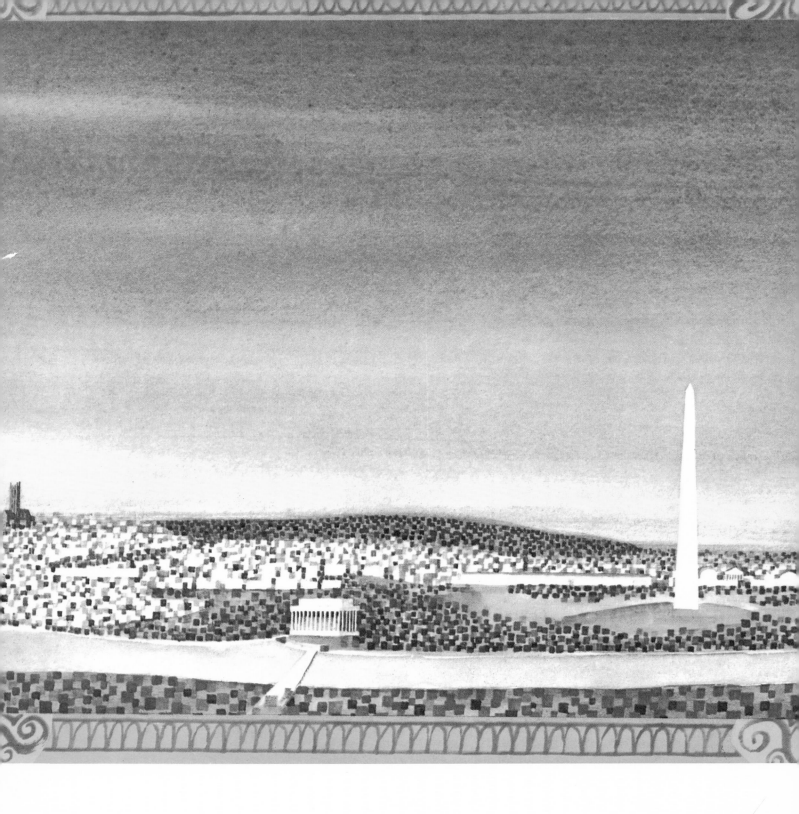

This is Washington, D.C., the capital of the United States of America. Situated on the Potomac River, it is a city of parks whose broad avenues, reminiscent of Paris, are lined with severe white porticoes of classic Roman dignity. Washington's first and foremost resident is Uncle Sam. It is the seat of the U.S. federal government. The Congress meets here, the president lives here, the Supreme Court sits here, foreign ambassadors reside here. Most business in Washington is government business and the government is everybody's business. Nearly one-third of the one million Washingtonians work for the government full time, and one half talk about it most of the time.

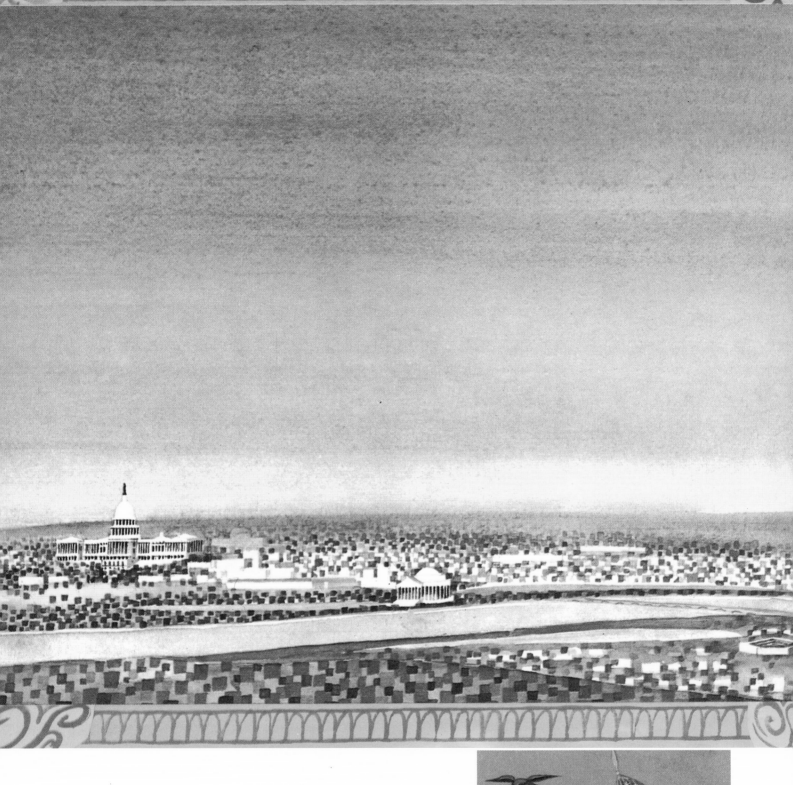

Miss Columbia was an early and successful competitor of Uncle Sam as a symbol of America. She is still remembered in the name Washington, D.C.—District of Columbia. The poets called America "Columbia" after the Italian explorer, Columbus, who discovered the New World.

Washington was named for the first president of the United States. A general and the commander in chief in the War of Independence, George Washington was elected president in 1789. He selected the site of the present capital but was the only president who never lived there. The presidential residence was not yet finished at the time of his death.

The Corcoran Gallery of Art.

Since many states wanted the "Federal City," as they then called it, to be on their territory, the decision was made to create a special district belonging to no state. In 1790 the District of Columbia was carved out of land originally part of Virginia and Maryland. The planning of the city was entrusted to a brilliant young French architect and engineer, Pierre Charles L'Enfant, who had served under Lafayette in the American Revolution. The Congress gave him a free hand, and he made Washington a city of spaceful, graceful vistas.

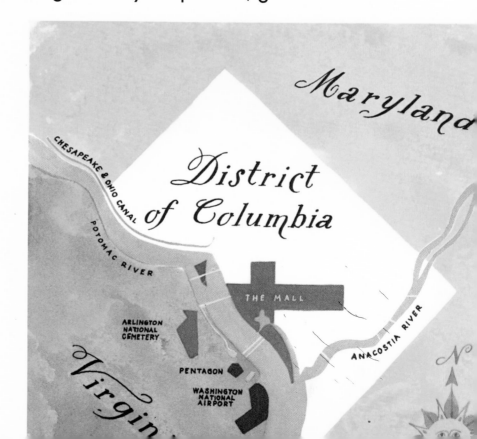

The Washington Monument commemorates the founder of the city. It serves as a beacon to the tourist. The monument is in the middle of the Mall and visible everywhere in the city. It is the world's tallest masonry structure, 555 feet high. Its cornerstone was laid in 1848, and after several interruptions its construction was finished some forty years later.

For a dime you can go up to the top of the monument, and you can either brave the steps (all 898 of them) or take an elevator.*

The windows face the four cardinal points of the compass, and you can see the panorama of the whole city.

But you don't have to walk very far from the monument to see the famous sights.

Nearly all are around the Mall.

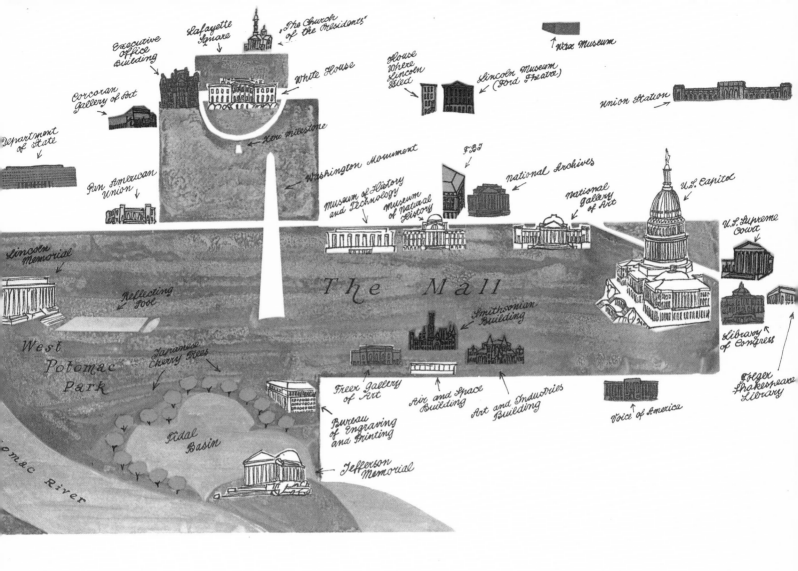

The Mall is a two-mile stretch of parkland in the heart of the city. Most of the museums, monuments, and memorials are there. And all the renowned federal buildings are nearby.

The men of the U.S. Park Police are always ready to ride to the rescue of a lost sightseer.

Many times as many tourists visit Washington every year as there are local inhabitants. They spend more time shooting Washington with their cameras than did the British shooting it with cannons in the War of 1812. Washington photographs well, and it's open house for the tourists in many federal buildings.

Washington's best season is spring, when the Japanese cherry trees around the Tidal Basin and the Jefferson Memorial are in bloom, and when Washington celebrates its famous Cherry Blossom Festival. Tokyo presented the trees to Washington at the beginning of this century. Some of the original 3,000 still bloom every year.

Summer in Washington is very hot—

and the winter is cold.

But Washington is ready for both.

Washington has many means of transportation.

But street names can be a bit confusing.

Some streets are numbered, some are lettered, some have names. And, roaming around Washington, you can find yourself in four different streets with the same name or letter as you go from one quadrant of the city to another.

It is all very logical, really, and a chess champion would probably get the hang of the system at once. You just keep looking for the tip of the Washington Monument.

14

Let's go to the Hill.

The Hill, of course, to Washingtonians means Capitol Hill. And the Capitol is the building that houses the Congress of the United States. The Senate meets in the Capitol's north wing, the House of Representatives in the south wing. Joint sessions of the Congress are held in the chamber of the House. The states are represented in the House of Representatives on the basis of their population: the more populous a state, the more representatives. But each state has just two senators. The Congress shares power with the president and the Supreme Court.

Besides their offices, the lawmakers have everything in the Capitol, from a watch repair shop to the best bean soup in town, served in their cafeteria.

From the top of the Capitol's dome, the *Statue of Freedom* supervises the nation's top lawmakers.

On the Hill, too, is the U.S. Supreme Court. It is built in the style of a classic Greek temple. Its columns are of white Vermont marble, which turns golden in the afternoon sun. It was designed by Cass Gilbert and completed in 1935. Formerly, the Supreme Court met in the Capitol. The nine Supreme Court justices are the supreme interpreters of the Constitution. If they hold a law to be unconstitutional, that's the end of that law. They meet from October to June.

At the lawmakers' disposition is the Library of Congress with its 41 million items.* It contains books, manuscripts, maps, films, photographs, sheet music, records. Only its computers can keep track of it all. Among its unique possessions, displayed on the main floor, is Jefferson's original draft of the Declaration of Independence and one copy of the first book ever printed, the Gutenberg Bible.

In front of the Folger Shakespeare Library you'll find this quotation from the Bard: "Lord, what fools these mortals be." But none of his admirers should be fools enough not to visit the library on their trip to Washington, for it has the finest collection of Shakespeariana a mortal has ever seen.

Shakespeare's plays have been produced all over the globe, but the Globe Theatre in London produced them first. It was Shakespeare's own theater. This is a small-scale model.

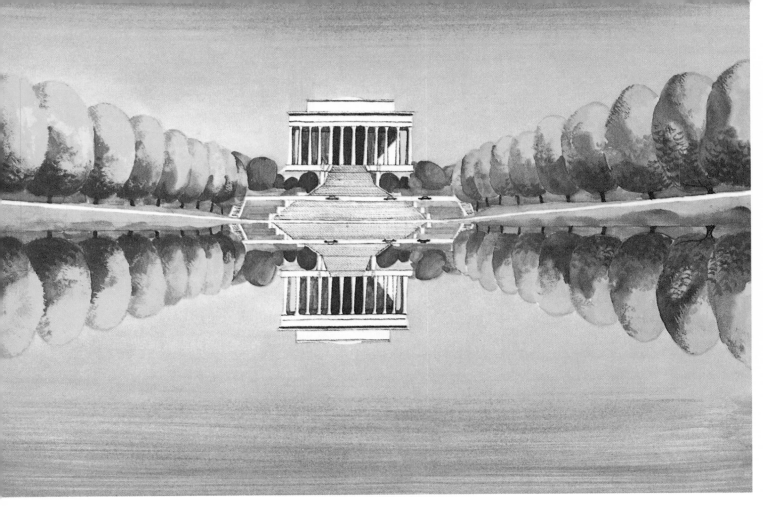

On the opposite side of the Mall is the Lincoln Memorial reflected in the Reflecting Pool. It is in the West Potomac Park, a spot where President Lincoln is said to have liked to walk alone at night. The memorial, designed by Henry Bacon, was dedicated in 1922. Its thirty-six marble columns represent the states of the Union which Lincoln held together.

Inside is the statue of Abraham Lincoln by Daniel Chester French. On the walls are inscribed two famous Lincoln speeches: his second inaugural address and his Gettysburg Address. Lincoln, the emancipator of slaves and the victorious leader of the Union in the Civil War, was assassinated on April 14, 1865.

Ford's Theatre, where Lincoln was shot, is now a Lincoln museum.

Opposite Ford's Theatre is the Petersen House, where the wounded president was carried and where he died. This house, too, is now a national memorial.

Among other historical tableaux, Lincoln's assassination by John Wilkes Booth can be seen in the National Historical Wax Museum.*

Every American is carrying bits and pieces of Washington in his pocket. The Lincoln Memorial is on a five-dollar bill. The bills themselves are made in Washington.

This is the Bureau of Engraving and Printing, which manufactures paper money and stamps. It started 150 years ago with six employees. Today, a few thousand persons work there; but of course people have more money today than they had a hundred years ago.

Here you see 10,000 sheets of white paper that will soon turn into greenbacks.*

Thirty-two notes are printed on every sheet. Six thousand in an hour.

After being checked, the sheets are separated in stacks of individual notes and wrapped for delivery. Each "brick" contains 4,000 notes.

It costs only one cent to make one dollar. Its lifetime is about thirteen months. Any time you walk through the glassed-in galleries of the Bureau, there may be 150 million dollars in paper money around you.*

The Jefferson Memorial was dedicated in 1943 on the 200th anniversary of the birth of Thomas Jefferson, one of the Founding Fathers of the Republic, the author of the Declaration of Independence, and one of America's most brilliant presidents. He was a philosopher of democracy, and many of his then-radical ideas have since become the common property of mankind.

Inside, quotations from Jefferson's writings are inscribed on four panels surrounding his 19-foot bronze statue. One reads: "I have sworn upon the altar of God eternal hostility against every form of tyranny over the mind of man."

Now let's cross the Mall again and visit the president. He lives in the White House. The White House got its name when its walls were whitewashed after the British had left it a charred ruin during the War of 1812. Tourists are welcome in Mr. President's house, but his living quarters on the second floor are not accessible. The White House has 132 rooms, 20 baths, and a swimming pool.

The president is the most powerful man in the United States, but not the best-paid one. His salary is $400,000, before taxes. And he earns every cent of it the hard way. His daily schedule is published every day in Washington papers.*

YESTERDAY

THE PRESIDENT

Signed the nuclear weapons treaty; received credentials from the Ambassador of Chile; participated in swearing in of Warren Smith as newly appointed member of the Council of Economic Advisers; received an award by the American Committee on Italian Migration for his immigration policy.

White House announced that the President would fly to El Salvador Saturday to attend a meeting of the Organization of Central American States.

Have you heard the latest?

And here you see Mr. President flying off on some business of state. His helicopter lifts off from the lawn of the garden behind the south lawn of the White House. No outsiders are allowed in the garden except children once a year for an Easter-egg-rolling party.* In the foreground is the Zero Milestone from which all the distances on D.C. roads are measured.

A few steps from the
White House, across
Lafayette Square, is
St. John's Church,
called "the Church
of the Presidents."

Inside, the President's Pew.

The State Department departed from this building some time ago, and now it is an executive building. The president sometimes holds his press conferences here. It is, in a way, an annex of the White House. The street between it and the Executive Building is blocked off and not accessible to the public.

DEPARTMENT
OF
STATE
2201 C STREET N.W.

The State Department recently moved to these bigger and better quarters to match the bigger U.S. involvement in world affairs. Besides helping the president to develop foreign policy, the State Department issues passports, runs the Peace Corps, and maintains liaison with the U.N.

The Pan American Union is the permanent secretariat of the Organization of American States. The building of the secretariat is owned by all the 35 states of the OAS. Its most beautiful feature is the patio with trees from South America: a coffee tree, a rubber tree, a banana plant, and many others.

This is not an imported Scottish castle. This is the headquarters of the Smithsonian Institution, a museum complex on the Mall. James Smithson, a British scientist, left his fortune to the United States to establish in Washington an institution for the "increase and diffusion of knowledge among men." There are some 143 million items in the Smithsonian Institution.

In the Arts and Industries Building and the Air and Space Museum, you can see everything that flies. Outside there are rockets and missiles—*

—and balloons, too, some days.

Inside, there are historical planes.

The *Spirit of St. Louis*, the plane flown by Charles Lindbergh on the first solo crossing of the Atlantic in 1927.

The Freer Gallery of Art, also a Smithsonian museum, has a magnificent collection of Asian art.

Don't be afraid of this "Guardian" at the entrance. He is made of wood and he is nearly 1,000 years old. He's as Japanese as the cherry trees.

Across the Mall is the National Museum of American History.

Inside, you'll see the original Star-Spangled Banner. It was the flag that flew over Baltimore's Fort McHenry in the War of 1812. Joyous that the British hadn't taken the fort, Francis Scott Key wrote a poem, "The Star-Spangled Banner." It was then set to music and became the U.S. national anthem.

The Senate Subway car, which ran between the Capitol and the Senate Office Building from 1915 to 1961, when it was replaced by a later model. It made an average of 225 trips a day. Capacity: 18 passengers.

A mid-nineteenth-century Pioneer locomotive.

As you walk toward the Museum of Natural History, you'll first meet this impressive creature with an impressive name: *Triceratops prorsus*. But you don't have to be in awe of him; he's a fake; he's made of cement.*

But there is a real one inside.

There are so many young visitors in all the museums that some teachers and excursion leaders mark their groups so they won't end up with more (or less) children than they began with. As you see, they wear different identifications.

There are some pretty weighty phenomena of nature in the museum. This elephant, the biggest ever shot, weighs twelve tons.

But that's nothing compared to this blue whale, which weighs sixty tons. Or did when caught. For this is its fiberglass mock-up. It is not real.*

But the blue diamond is. It is called the Hope Diamond. It weighs 45 ½ carats. And that's a whale of a diamond.

This is the Museum of Natural History.

In the National Gallery of Art, you will find a painting by just about every famous artist whose name you can recall.

A Girl with a Watering Can by Auguste Renoir (Chester Dale Collection, National Gallery of Art).

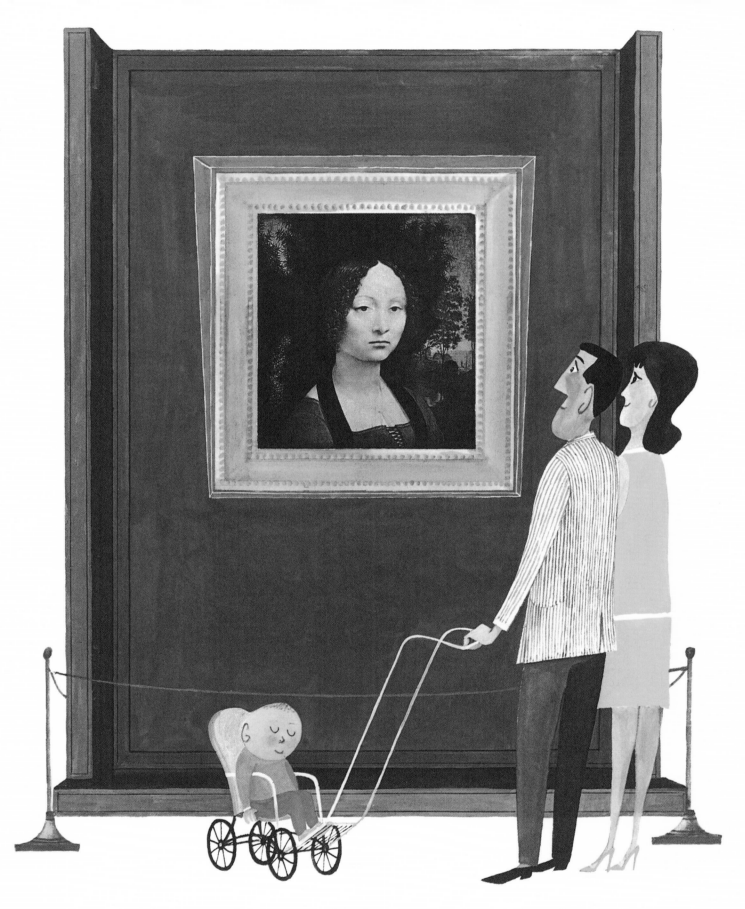

Ginevra de' Benci by Leonardo da Vinci (National Gallery of Art, Ailsa Mellon Bruce Fund).

Older art lovers are offered a guide. Tiny art lovers are offered free transport.

In the National Zoological Park, which also belongs to the Smithsonian Institution, you can get a look at two celebrities.

The white tiger, presented by an Indian maharaja to President Eisenhower as a gift to American children. She is the only white tiger in captivity. Her name: "Mohini Rewa"— the Enchantress of Rewa.*

Meet Smokey the Bear, who appeals to Americans on posters to prevent forest fires. Smokey was rescued from a forest fire in New Mexico by rangers in 1950, and since then has lived in Washington. His fur is a rusty brown, but nonetheless his name is American Black Bear. He is behind a glass panel. No autographs.*

The most important national documents are preserved in the National Archives. Among them is the original of the Declaration of Independence, the Bill of Rights, and the Constitution.

In the Rotunda these precious documents, sealed in bronze and glass cases, are protected from harmful light by special filters.

The Department of Justice on Pennsylvania Avenue.

Here is also the national headquarters of the Federal Bureau of Investigation, better known as the FBI. An FBI guide will show you the pictures of the ten most-wanted men, exhibits from famous spy cases, and captured arsenals of notorious gangsters.* The FBI has more than 250 million fingerprints on file in the Identification Division.

At the end of the tour, G-men show their marksmanship. But on duty they are allowed to use this skill only for defending themselves or to save lives.

The Department of Health and Human Services is the home of the Voice of America. Let's go for a tour around its studios.

The Voice of America broadcasts information about American political and cultural life in forty-four languages to millions of listeners and viewers all over the world.

There are twenty-seven studios and four television studios, and from each you can hear and see broadcasts in different languages.

The Master Control.

The Voice of America started during World War II, and its first broadcast was in German. It said: "The news may be good or bad. But we shall tell you the truth." This has been its policy ever since.

The Department of Defense.

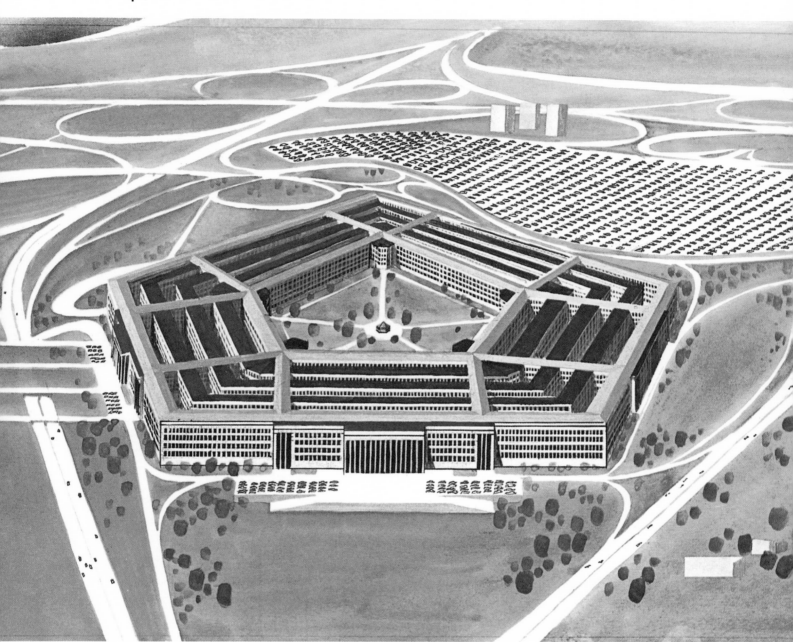

This is the Pentagon, the top command post of the U.S. armed forces. Just to march across one of its several immense parking lots toward the entrance can give you a bad case of battle fatigue. The Pentagon got its name from its geometric design, but its name has become synonymous with the U.S. military top brass, for the Joint Chiefs of Staff of the Army, the Navy, the Air Force, and the Marine Corps have their offices there. But there are some 23,000 others working in the Pentagon building. The commander in chief of this huge military machine, however, is a civilian: the president of the United States. The secretary of defense, too, is a civilian and his office is here.

Georgetown is the oldest part of Washington, a district of beautiful old houses as well as of cozy small taverns and bookshops: an exclusive residential area and also an artists' quarter. Georgetown used to be a port. It is the eastern terminus of the Chesapeake and Ohio Canal. By the way, it is named for George II, the British king, not George Washington, the American president.

In Georgetown, there are many strange visitors.

Arlington National Cemetery.

Veterans of all the wars the U.S. has fought are buried here. On simple tombstones you can read the names of admirals next to those of seamen, of generals buried side by side with their men and women. Astronauts' graves are also at Arlington Cemetery.

But most visitors first pay their respects at the grave of President John F. Kennedy. His brother, Senator Robert F. Kennedy, is buried nearby.

Not far from the cemetery entrance is the U.S. Marine Corps War Memorial. The most famous news photo from World War II was the model for the memorial. It represents the flag raising on Mount Suribachi on the island of Iwo Jima. In that battle, 6,800 Marines died, and more than 20,000 Japanese. Iwo Jima was returned to Japan in 1968.

The statue of President Andrew Jackson in Lafayette Square.

"Goodbye, Mr. President! Could you tell the other Mr. President I liked seeing Washington?" "Certainly. He lives just across the street, and we see each other every time he looks out the window."

THIS IS WASHINGTON, D.C. . . . TODAY!

* **PAGE 8:** Today, tickets to go to the top of the Washington Monument are distributed free of charge! Lines form early in the morning, and they run out quickly during the spring and summer months.

* **PAGE 19:** The largest library in the world, today the Library of Congress stores 145 million items on approximately 745 miles of bookshelves.

* **PAGE 25:** The National Historical Wax Museum is no longer there, but you can visit Madame Tussauds in Washington, D.C., where you'll see many historical and political figures—including Abraham Lincoln!

* **PAGE 26:** The Bureau of Engraving and Printing (BEP) is still the only producer of U.S. currency, but it stopped making postage stamps in 2005. The "paper money" isn't really paper—it is made of linen and cotton; and it isn't really white—it also contains red and blue fibers. "Greenbacks" are no longer printed with just black and green ink, either. The notes have subtle background colors and "symbols of freedom," which are different for each denomination.

* **PAGE 27:** Today, BEP presses can print 10,000 sheets per hour. It costs almost five cents to print a one-dollar bill (higher denominations cost more), and its lifespan is twenty-one months. It produces about 26 million notes a day, worth a total of 907 million dollars.

* **PAGE 30:** Today, the origin of the "White House" name is up for debate. One theory is that it was named after Martha Washington's home, White House Plantation in Virginia. In addition, the president's schedule is no longer printed in the daily newspapers, but it does appear on some political websites.

* **PAGE 32:** Today, visitors are welcome every spring to view the Jacqueline Kennedy Garden, the Rose Garden, the Children's Garden, and the South Lawn of the White House. And since Michelle Obama and a group of elementary students planted a vegetable garden at the White House in 2009, children have been invited to attend a "kitchen garden tour."

* **PAGE 36:** The Arts and Industries Building closed for renovation in 2004. Today, the Air and Space Museum collection is housed in a different Smithsonian building.

* **PAGE 41:** The dinosaur that used to sit outside of the Museum of Natural History has been moved to the National Zoo. Today, the museum has a bronze cast of the skull of a *Triceratops horridus* outside the south entrance.

* **PAGE 42:** The model of the blue whale was removed from the museum in 2000. It was replaced by a 45-foot, 2,300-pound, full-scale model of the Atlantic right whale (*Eubalaena glacialis*), which is the centerpiece of the new Sant Ocean Hall.

* **PAGE 46:** Today, the most celebrated animals at the National Zoo are the giant pandas. The current pair, Mei Xiang and Tian Tian, has lived there since 2000.

* **PAGE 47:** Thousands of people visited Smokey the Bear at the National Zoo. After he retired in 1975, "Little Smokey" carried on his tradition of greeting zoo visitors until 1990.

* **PAGE 50:** The FBI tour has been discontinued since 2001. The International Spy Museum, dedicated to espionage, has offered a fun alternative for visitors since it opened in 2002.

The National Air and Space Museum has the world's largest collection of historic air- and spacecraft, including the *Spirit of St. Louis*, the Apollo II module, and the Wright brothers' first airplane.

The giant pandas are the most celebrated animals today at the National Zoo.

After learning about the many tribes at the National Museum of the American Indian, you can sample some traditional foods like frybread and *totopos* in the café.

Choose a "cover" when you enter the International Spy Museum, for access into the world of top secret espionage.

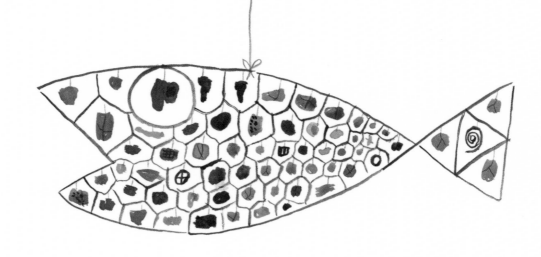

The Hirshhorn Museum and Sculpture Garden collection has many interesting sculptures, such as Alexander Calder's colorful *Fish*.

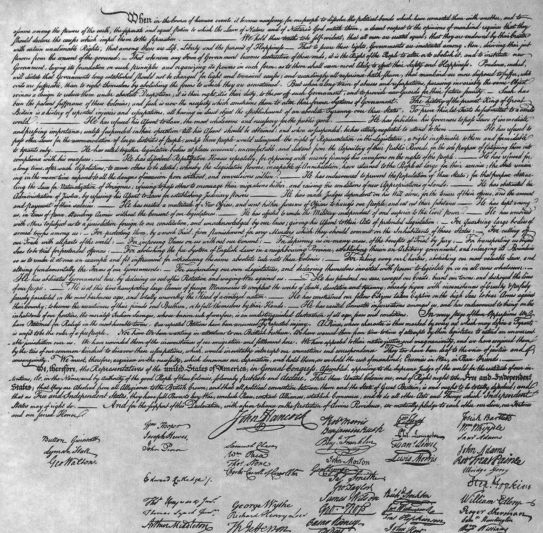